Girl's Guide to Cooking

JG
PRESS

Published in 2011 by
World Publications Group, Inc.
140 Laurel Street,
East Bridgewater, MA 02333
www.wrldpub.com

C005 0111
10 9 8 7 6 5 4 3 2 1

ISBN: 978-1-57215-7712

Printed and manufactured in China

Contents

Introduction

Welcome to the wonderful world of cookery! If you're a beginner, a super chef, or you just love food, try making some delicious, mouth-watering recipes to make your taste buds tingle.

There are four great sections for you to choose from: afternoon treats, and snacks, baking, delicious dishes and desserts. There are scrumptious recipes that are perfect for tea parties, special birthdays and perfect lunchbox snacks like butterfly buns, chocolate cupcakes, or banana muffins. You can make your own ice-cream, or classic recipes like fish and chips and spaghetti and meatballs. With simple ingredients and easy-to-follow recipes, you will find helpful hints and tips along the way, so you can master making tasty treats and meals for you and your whole family!

To begin, read the golden rules carefully and learn the symbols on the opposite page. Then, it's time to get cooking!

Golden Rules

1. Always ask an adult's permission before you start cooking, or ask them to help you.
2. Wash your hands.
3. To keep your clothes clean, wear an apron.
4. Measure your ingredients carefully.
5. Use a separate chopping board if you're cutting meat.
6. Take extra care with scissors or knives; ask an adult to teach you or to help.
7. Always use oven gloves and be careful when using the oven.
8. When you've finished, help clean the kitchen and wash the dishes.

Symbols

Portion size

Preparation and cook time

Difficulty

easy   medium   hard

Afternoon
treats and snacks

serves
2

15 mins

preparation and cooking time

difficulty

French toast with fresh berries

Method

Mix the eggs, milk and 1 tbsp sugar in a shallow dish. Add the bread, then turn the slices in the liquid until they are well soaked.

Melt the butter in a large frying pan over a low heat, then add the slices of bread and fry on each side until golden brown.

Put a slice on each plate, sprinkle with the remaining sugar and spoon over the berries.

Ingredients

2 eggs, beaten
100 ml / 3.4 oz / ½ cup milk
30 g / 1 oz / ¼ cup caster sugar
4 slices bread
50 g / 1.8 oz / ½ cup butter
200 g / 7 oz / 2 cups mixed fresh berries

Why not try...
dipping the fruit into chocolate.

Banana smoothie with cinnamon

Method

Put the bananas, milk, honey and ice into a blender and blend until smooth.

Pour into glasses and sprinkle with the ground cinnamon.

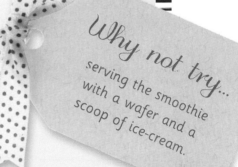

Why not try...
serving the smoothie with a wafer and a scoop of ice-cream.

Ingredients

4 bananas, sliced
1.1 litre / 37.2 fl. oz / 4 ⅔ cups milk
4 tbsp honey
6 ice cubes, crushed
1½ tsp ground cinnamon

Sticky muesli bars

Method

Heat the oven to 180C (155 fan) 350F, gas 4. Line a rectangular baking tin with non-stick baking paper.

With the help of an adult, heat the butter, sugar and golden syrup in a pan on a low heat until just melted.

Add the muesli and mix well. Tip into the baking tin and spread evenly.

Bake for 15-20 minutes, remove it from the oven and mark into 12 bars and leave it to cool completely in the tin, as it falls apart when warm. Cut it into bars when it has cooled.

30 mins

preparation and cooking time

difficulty

Ingredients

110 g / 3.9 oz / 1 cup butter
85 g / 3 oz / ¾ cup light brown sugar
75 g / 2.6 oz / ¾ cup golden syrup
275 g / 9.7 oz / 2¾ cups muesli

Top tip...

you can add nuts, fruit, or even chocolate chips!

4

40 mins

preparation and cooking time

difficulty

Chunky oven chips

Method

Heat the oven to 200C (175 fan) 400F, gas 6.

Wash and dry the potatoes, but don't peel them. Cut the potatoes into wedges and place in a large bowl.

Add the remaining ingredients to the bowl and mix until the potatoes are well coated. Tip the potatoes onto a baking tray.

Bake for 30-40 minutes until golden brown and cooked all the way through.

Ingredients

1 kg / 2 lbs / 10 cups potatoes
2 tbsp olive oil
sea salt
freshly ground black pepper
paprika, optional

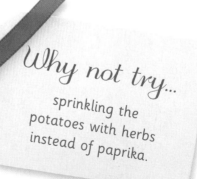

Why not try...
sprinkling the potatoes with herbs instead of paprika.

Coconut ice bars

Method

Butter a tin 20 cm x 15 cm / 8" x 6".

Carefully heat the icing sugar and condensed milk in a pan over a low heat until the sugar has completely dissolved.

Remove from the heat and stir in the coconut. Quickly pour half of the mixture into the tin. Leave it to cool for 5 minutes.

Add a few drops of colouring to the second half, mix well and pour over the first layer. When the coconut ice is half set, carefully mark into bars with a knife. Once it has completely cooled, cut it into bars.

20 mins

preparation and cooking time

difficulty

Ingredients

340 g / 12 oz / 3½ cups icing (confectioners') sugar
400 g / 14.1 oz / 4 cups condensed milk
340 g / 12 oz / 3½ cups desiccated coconut
red food colouring

Top tip...
coconut ice makes a great snack for your lunchbox.

makes

16

30 mins

preparation and cooking time

difficulty

Muesli biscuits

Method

Heat the oven to 180C (155 fan) 350F, gas 4. Grease a baking tray with a little bit of butter to make sure the biscuits don't stick.

Mix the muesli, flour and sugar in a mixing bowl. Make a well in the centre and add the honey, egg and butter and mix well.

Drop tablespoonfuls of the mixture onto the baking tray, pressing down lightly with the back of a floured spoon.

Bake for 15-20 minutes until lightly golden. Allow the biscuits to cool for 5 minutes, then remove from the baking tray and cool completely on a wire rack.

Ingredients

300 g / 10.5 oz / 3 cups muesli
120 g / 4.2 oz / 1¼ cups self-raising flour
100 g / 3.5 oz / 1 cup light brown sugar
100 g / 3.5 oz / 1 cup butter, melted
3 tbsp honey
1 egg, beaten

Why not try...
making bigger cookies with the dough instead of small biscuits.

Strawberry shake

preparation and cooking time
10 mins

Method

Put all the ingredients into a blender and blend until it is smooth.

Pour into chilled glasses. Add ice cubes if you wish.

If the milkshake is too runny, try adding more yoghurt. If natural yoghurt is too sour, you can add vanilla or strawberry yoghurt.

difficulty

Ingredients

200 g | 7 oz | 2 cups strawberries, halved
100 g | 3.5 oz | 1 cup natural yoghurt
300 ml | 10 fl. oz | 1¼ cups milk
1 dash lemon juice
2 tbsp honey

Top tip...
you can make shakes with any fruit you like! Try raspberries, blueberries, or even mangoes.

Top tip...
try different fillings
like tomatoes, mushrooms,
or potatoes.

Cheesy filo pastries with red onion

makes

10

50 mins

preparation and cooking time

difficulty

Method

Heat the oven to 180C (155 fan) 350F, gas 4. Rub a little bit of butter on to a baking tray to stop the pastries sticking when they cook.

Carefully heat 2 tablespoons of the oil in a frying pan over a medium heat. Cook the chopped onion for 5 minutes, stirring regularly. Add the oregano, salt and pepper and remove the pan from the heat. Stir in the feta cheese and set the mixture aside to cool.

Carefully melt the butter in a small pan over a low heat. Once it has melted, take it off the heat and mix in the rest of the olive oil.

Using a sharp knife or scissors, cut the pastry sheets lengthwise into 6 cm / 2½" wide strips.

Place one strip on a flat surface and brush it lightly with the melted butter and oil mixture, then place a level tablespoon of the feta filling at one end. Fold the end of the strip over the filling so that it forms a triangle shape. Continue folding, until it is a sealed, triangular-shaped parcel.

Brush the outside of the panel with the oil mixture. Repeat the process until you have used all the feta filling. Place the parcels on the baking tray and cook for 20-25 minutes until crispy and golden.

Ingredients

250 g / 8.8 oz / 2½ cups filo pastry
5 tbsp olive oil
1 red onion, chopped
½ tsp dried oregano
½ tsp salt
¼ tsp freshly ground black pepper
110 g / 3.9 oz / 1 cup feta cheese, crumbled
2 tbsp melted butter

Assorted yoghurts with berries, melon and cereal

Method

Spoon the yoghurt into a bowl. You can combine as many flavours of yoghurt as you want to.

Next, choose as many of the toppings as you like. Try fresh fruit, or mixed nuts and honey swirled into the yoghurt, or cereal sprinkled over the top.

For a special treat, mix chocolate spread into the yoghurt and top with crunchy nuts.

Ingredients

fruit or natural yoghurt

Suggested toppings:
strawberries, sliced
banana, sliced
blueberries
melon, cubed
cereal
nuts
honey
jam
chocolate spread
fruit puree

Why not try...
taking yoghurt pots to school as a tasty treat.

35 mins

preparation and cooking time

difficulty

Fudge bars

Method

Rub a little bit of butter onto a deep baking tray so the fudge doesn't stick.

Make sure an adult is helping you, as sugar is very hot when it melts. Mix the sugar, water, butter and condensed milk together in a tall pot or pan, because the mixture rises quickly, and bring to a gentle boil, on a low heat.

While the mixture is gently boiling, stir it continuously with a wooden spoon for half an hour, to make sure no sugar sticks to the bottom of the pot. The fudge will become thick, sticky and turn dark brown.

Once it looks ready, take the pan off the boil. Add the vanilla essence, and beat the mixture very well for a minute, then pour the mixture into the baking tray and allow it to cool completely.

Ingredients

400 g / 14.1 oz / 4 cups condensed milk
500g / 17.6 oz / 5 cups caster sugar
120ml / 4 fl. oz / ½ cup water
50 g / 1.7 oz / ½ cup butter
2 tsp vanilla essence

Why not try...
adding sultanas or peanuts to the fudge.

Baking

Top tip...
decorate with icing sugar,
chocolate chips, marshmallows,
or sprinkles!

Chocolate cupcakes

Method

Heat the oven to 200C (175 fan) 400F, gas 6.
Arrange 12 paper cases in a bun tin.

Sift the flour, sugar, baking powder and salt into
a mixing bowl.

Whisk together the egg, milk, oil and vanilla.
Stir into the dry ingredients until everything
is smooth and well mixed.

Spoon the mixture into the paper cases and bake
for 20 minutes until golden. Allow the cupcakes
to cool in the tin for 5 minutes, then place on
a wire rack and cool completely.

For the chocolate topping, heat the cream in
a pan on a low heat and bring it almost to
boiling point. Remove the pan from the heat and
stir in the chocolate until melted. Leave it to cool
and thicken. If it is too runny, try adding a little
cream cheese and mix well.

Spoon the topping onto each cup cake.

difficulty

Ingredients

For the cupcakes:
225 g / 7.9 oz / 2¼ cups
plain (all-purpose) flour
90 g / 3.1 oz / 1 cup caster sugar
2 tsp baking powder
pinch of salt
1 egg, beaten
150 ml / 5 fl. oz / ⅔ cup milk
50 ml / 1.7 fl. oz / ¼ cup sunflower oil
1 tsp vanilla extract

For the chocolate topping:
150 ml / 5 fl. oz cup / ⅔ cup cream
150 g / 5.2 oz plain or milk chocolate
cream cheese (optional)

Why not try...
using white chocolate chips or marshmallows.

Chocolate chip and coconut biscuits

difficulty

Method

Heat the oven to 180C (155 fan) 350F, gas 4. Rub a little bit of butter over 2 baking trays to stop the biscuits from sticking.

Mix the butter and both sugars until soft and smooth. Beat in the egg and vanilla.

Sift the flour into the bowl, followed by the baking powder and salt and beat well until everything is combined. Stir in the chocolate chips and coconut.

Drop teaspoons of the mixture onto the baking trays, spacing them 5 cm / 2" apart. Flatten them lightly with a wet fork.

Carefully place the baking trays in the oven and bake for 10-12 minutes until the biscuits are golden. Place the biscuits on a wire rack to cool completely.

Ingredients

75 g / 2.6 oz / ¾ cup butter
110 g / 3.5 oz / 1 cup caster sugar
50 g / 1.8 oz / ½ cup light brown sugar
1 egg
1 tsp vanilla extract
110 g / 3.5 oz / 1 cup plain (all-purpose) flour
1 tsp baking powder
pinch of salt
125 g / 4.4 oz / 1¼ cup chocolate chips
50 g / 1.8 oz ½ cup desiccated coconut

makes

12

30 mins

preparation and cooking time

difficulty

Strawberry banana muffins

Method

Heat the oven to 190C (165 fan) 375F, gas 5. Put 12 paper cases in a muffin tin.

Melt the butter in a pan over a low heat. In a mixing bowl, stir the sugar, yoghurt, melted butter and eggs together.

Sift together the flour, baking powder, bicarbonate of soda and salt into another bowl.

Pour the egg mixture into the dry ingredients and mix gently. Quickly stir in the banana and strawberries. Do not over-mix, the mixture will be lumpy because of the fruit.

Spoon the mixture into the paper cases and bake for 15-20 minutes, until golden. Test with a wooden toothpick, if it comes out clean, the muffins are done.

Ingredients

350 g / 12.3 oz / 3½ cups plain (all-purpose) flour
1 tbsp baking powder
½ tsp bicarbonate of soda
pinch of salt
175 g / 6.2 oz / 1¾ cups caster sugar
250 g / 8.8 oz / 2½ cups natural yoghurt
100 g / 3.5 oz / 1 cup butter, melted
2 eggs, beaten
1 large banana, peeled and diced
150 g / 5.3 oz / 1½ cups strawberries, sliced

Top tip...
these muffins are
great for tea parties!

Top tip...
use different shaped
cutters to make stars, hearts,
or gingerbread people.

Gingerbread Easter bunnies

difficulty

Method

Heat the oven to 180C (160 fan) 350F, gas mark 4.

Heat the honey, sugar and butter in a pan on a low heat, stirring, until the sugar has dissolved. Remove the pan from the heat and pour it into a bowl, letting it cool down.

Add the ground almonds, flour, spices, lemon zest and egg to the butter bowl and mix well. Stir in the bicarbonate of soda and water and continue kneading until the dough is shiny and does not stick to the bowl. Add a little more flour if needed, to form a dough.

Roll out the dough on a floured board with a rolling pin, to a thickness of 4-5 mm and cut out Easter bunnies using a cutter. Place on the baking trays and bake for 14-18 minutes. Carefully remove from the oven, and slide them off the baking tray on to a wire rack to cool.

Mix the icing sugar with enough water and lemon juice to make a creamy icing. Put it into an icing bag, or plastic food bag, and snip off a corner to make a small hole, and decorate the Easter Bunnies. Leave to dry.

Ingredients

For the dough:
250 ml / 8.4 fl. oz / 1 cup honey
250 g / 8.4 oz / 2½ cups brown sugar
150 g / 5.2 oz / 1½ cups butter
100 g / 3.5 oz / 1 cup ground almonds
400 g / 14.1 / 4 cups
plain (all-purpose) flour
1 tsp ground cinnamon
¼ tsp ground cloves
¼ tsp ground cardamom
¼ tsp ground mixed spice
4 tsp ground ginger
2 tsp finely grated lemon zest
1 egg
1 tsp bicarbonate of soda
2 tbsp water
flour, for the work surface

To decorate:
200 g / 7 oz / 2 cups icing sugar
2 tbsp lemon juice
a little water

difficulty

Rose and lychee cupcakes

Method

Heat the oven to 180C (155 fan) 350F, gas 4. Place 12 cupcake cases in a bun tin.

Take the skins and pits from the lychees and puree them in a blender with the milk and vanilla extract.

Mix the butter and sugar until it is soft and smooth. Add the egg and egg whites and mix until it is just combined.

Sift in the flour, baking powder and salt and stir until combined. Add the lychee mixture and mix well.

Spoon the mixture into the cupcake cases and bake in the oven for 20-25 minutes until the tops are lightly golden. Test with a wooden toothpick, if it comes out clean, the cupcakes are done. Leave to them to cool for 10 minutes, then place on a wire rack to cool completely.

For the icing, whisk the butter with an electric whisk until it is soft and creamy. Gradually mix in the sugar and milk, followed by the rose water and colouring, and then beat until smooth.

Spoon the frosting onto the cupcakes and smooth it evenly and top each cupcake with a rose petal for decoration.

Ingredients

180 ml / 6 fl. oz / ¾ cup lychees, fresh or tinned
60 ml / 2 oz / ¼ cup milk
½ tsp vanilla extract
110 g / 3.9 oz / 1 cup butter
200 g / 7 oz / 2 cups caster sugar
1 egg
2 egg whites
200 g / 7 oz / 2 cups
plain (all-purpose) flour
1 tsp baking powder
¼ tsp salt

For the icing:
140 g / 4.9 oz / 1½ cups
unsalted butter
110 g / 3.9 oz / 1 cup
icing (confectioners') sugar, sifted
2 tsp milk
½ tsp rose water
2 - 3 drops pink colouring

Top tip...
these cupcakes are perfect
for birthday parties!

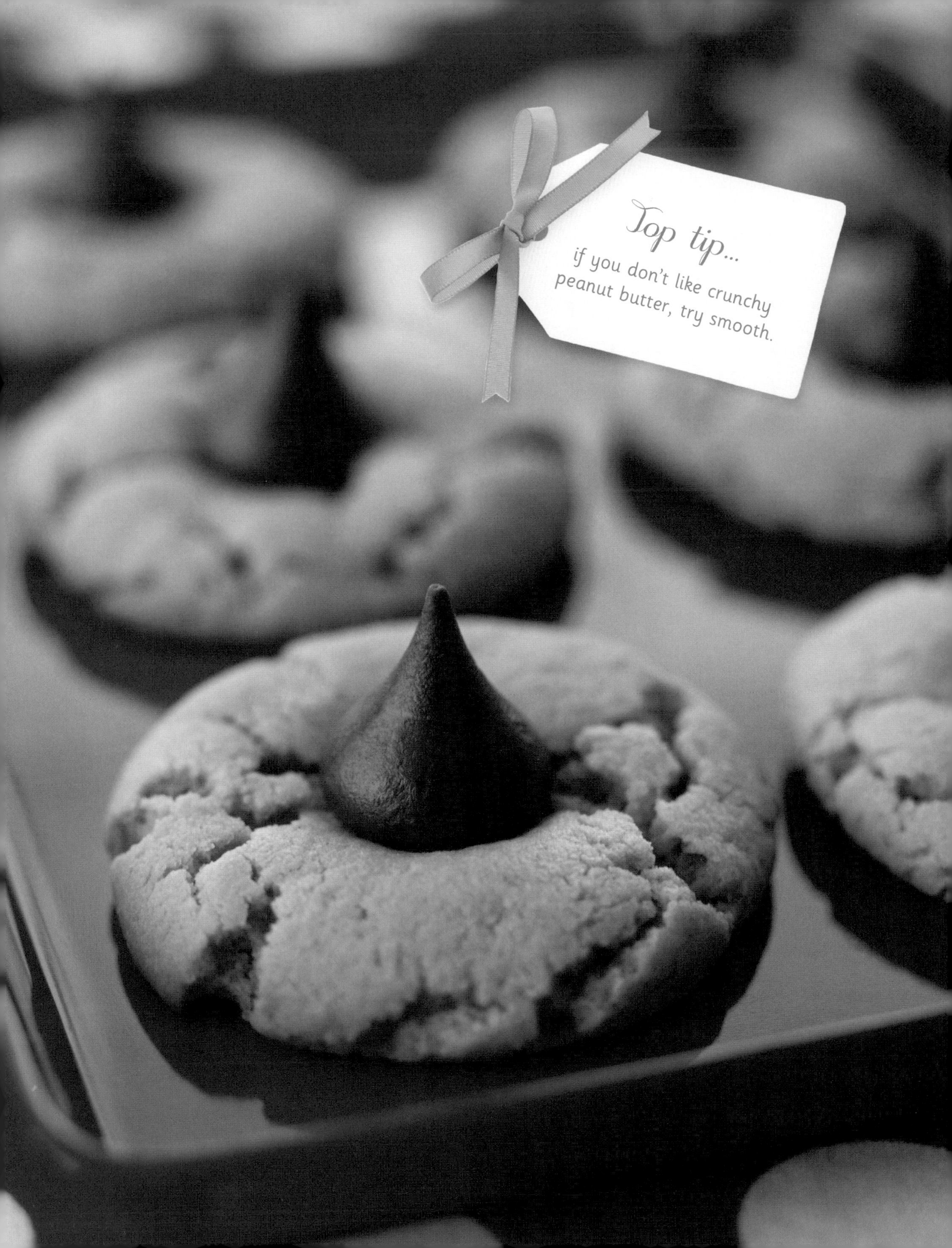
Top tip...
if you don't like crunchy
peanut butter, try smooth.

Peanut butter kiss cookies

Method

Heat the oven to 180C (155 fan) 350F, gas 4. Mix the butter and sugar until soft and smooth. Mix the egg with the vanilla and gradually beat into the butter mixture. Stir in the peanut butter until everything is well mixed.

Sift in the flour, bicarbonate of soda and mix to form a dough. Place the bowl in the refrigerator for 30 minutes so the dough is firm.

Rub a little bit of butter over 2 baking trays to stop the cookies from sticking.

Spoon out teaspoons of the dough and roll into balls. Place the balls on the baking trays and press into flat rounds with a fork.

Bake for 10-12 minutes until golden. Allow the cookies to cool completely on a wire rack.

Using a piping bag, or a plastic food bag with the corner cut off, place a little chocolate spread on the centre of each cookie.

difficulty

Ingredients

110 g / 3.9 oz / 1 cup butter
125 g / 4.4 oz / 1¼ cup light brown sugar
1 egg
1 tsp vanilla extract
225 g / 7.9 oz / 2¼ cups crunchy peanut butter
110 g / 3.9 oz / 1 cup plain (all-purpose) flour
½ tsp bicarbonate of soda
7 tbsp chocolate spread

difficulty

Butterfly buns

Method

Heat the oven to 180C (160C fan) 375F, gas 5. Place 24 paper baking cups in a bun tin.

Beat the butter with the sugar until it is pale and fluffy. Add the eggs and cream cheese and mix well.

Sift the flour and baking powder into the mixture and stir until all the ingredients are blended.

Spoon the mixture into the paper cups. Carefully place the tray in the oven for 15-17 minutes. Once they're cooked through, let them cool on a wire rack.

For the icing, mix the icing sugar with the cream cheese and a few drops of food colouring, and a tablespoonful of water at a time, until the icing is smooth and thick. Carefully spoon the icing onto the buns and smooth it out evenly.

Halve the biscuits and arrange 2 halves on each bun to resemble butterfly wings. Dust with the remaining icing sugar.

Ingredients

For the dough:
125 g / 4.4 oz / 1¼ cups butter, softened
120 g / 4.2 oz / 1¼ cups sugar
2 eggs
200 g / 7 oz / 2 cups cream cheese, or quark
250 g / 8.8 oz / 2½ cups
plain (all-purpose) flour
3 tsp baking powder

To decorate:
red food colouring
3 tbsp icing (confectioners') sugar
150 g / 5.2 oz / 1½ cups cream cheese, or quark
24 small sponge biscuits, ready-made

Why not try...
adding mashed strawberries
to the icing instead
of food colouring.

makes

10

45 mins

preparation and cooking time

difficulty

Coconut and raspberry cake

Method

Heat the oven to 200C (175 fan) 400F, gas 6, and butter a rectangular baking tin.

Mix the flour, butter, sugar, eggs, salt and desiccated coconut together to form a dough. Wrap in clingfilm and put it in the refrigerator for 1 hour.

Roll out the dough with a floured rolling pin to a 1 cm / ⅜" thickness and place it in the tin, taking the dough up the sides of the tin.

Scatter the raspberries on the dough and sift over icing sugar to taste. Cover with the remaining coconut flakes.

Bake for 20-25 minutes or until nicely browned. Leave to cool, then cut into rectangles.

Ingredients

300 g / 10.5 oz / 3 cups plain (all-purpose) flour
200 g / 7 oz / 2 cups butter
100 g / 3.5 oz / 1 cup sugar
pinch of salt
2 eggs, beaten
300 g / 10.5 oz / 3 cups flaked coconut
500 g / 17.6 oz / 5 cups raspberries
icing (confectioners') sugar
150 g / 5.2 oz / 1½ cups desiccated coconut

Top tip...
this cake is perfect to have with a strawberry shake (see page 20).

Rock cakes

30 mins

preparation and cooking time

difficulty

Method

Heat the oven to 190C (165 fan) 375F, gas 5. Rub a bit of butter on a baking tray to make sure the cakes don't stick when they're cooking.

Sift the flour, salt and baking powder into a mixing bowl and rub in the butter until the mixture resembles breadcrumbs.

Stir in the sugar, fruit and spices. Beat in the egg and milk to make a stiff, doughy mixture.

Drop tablespoons of the mixture onto the baking tray and rough up each with a fork.

Bake for 15 to 20 minutes until cooked through. Carefully remove the tray from the oven and cool the cakes on a wire rack.

Top tip...
make these rock cakes the day before you need them so the outsides will be crunchier!

Ingredients

225 g / 7.9 oz / 1¼ cups plain (all-purpose) flour
75 g / 2.6 oz / ¾ cups butter
75 g / 2.6 oz / ¾ cups caster sugar
75 g / 2.6 oz / ¾ cups sultanas
2-3 tbsp milk
2 tsp baking powder
¼ tsp grated nutmeg
¼ tsp ground mixed spice
¼ tsp salt
1 egg, beaten

Scones with cream and jam

makes
12

30 mins
preparation and cooking time

difficulty

Method

Heat the oven to 220C (195 fan) 425F, gas 7. Use a little bit of butter to grease a baking tray and sprinkle some flour over the greased tray.

Sift the flour into a large mixing bowl. Lightly rub in the butter until the mixture resembles breadcrumbs.

Stir in the sugar and sultanas. Make a well in the centre and pour in the milk. Mix to a soft dough and put it on a floured surface.

Knead the dough with your hands until it is smooth and roll out to 1.5 cm / ¾" thickness. Cut out rounds using a 5 cm / 2" cookie cutter.

Place the scones on the baking tray and bake for 10-15 minutes, until they have risen and are golden. Allow them to cool on a wire rack and serve with whipped cream and jam.

Ingredients

225 g / 7.9 / 1¼ cups self-raising flour
50 g / 1.8 oz / ½ cup butter
50 g / 1.8 oz / ½ cup caster sugar
150 ml / 5 fl. oz / ⅔ cup oz milk
50 g / 1.8 oz / ½ cup sultanas

Top tip...

try making savoury scones by substituting the sultanas for 60 g / 2 oz / ½ cup of cheese.

Top tip...
chill the brownies in the tin, in the refrigerator, so they are easier to slice.

Coconut brownies

difficulty

Method

Heat the oven to 180C (155 fan) 350F, gas 4. Line the base of a 21 cm / 8" inch square tin with baking parchment.

Put the butter and sugar in a large pan and melt on a low heat, stirring so the mixture doesn't burn. When the mixture is melted, remove from the heat and leave it to cool slightly.

Stir in the eggs, a little at a time, followed by the flour. Place the chocolate in a bowl over a pan of simmering water, on a low heat until it is completely melted, stirring to make sure it doesn't burn.

Pour a third of the batter into a small bowl and stir in the coconut and coconut essence.

Stir the melted chocolate into the remaining batter and spread the batter evenly in the tin.

Spoon the coconut batter evenly over the chocolate layer, then spread carefully to form an even layer.

Place the baking tin in the oven for 30-35 minutes. Cool the brownies in the tin, then cut into squares or bars.

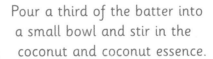

Ingredients

250 g / 8.8 oz / 2½ cups butter
500 g / 17.6 oz / 5 cups caster sugar
4 eggs, beaten
110 g / 3.9 oz / 1 cup self-raising flour
100 g / 3.5 oz / 1 cup flaked coconut
½ tsp coconut essence
110 g / 3.9 oz / 1 cup dark or milk chocolate

Delicious dishes

Chicken and mango wraps

Method

With the help of an adult, heat the oil in a wide pan and gently fry the chicken for 5 minutes on each side, or until golden brown and cooked through. Allow the meat to cool, then cut it up into small chunks or pull it apart.

Peel the mangoes and chop the fruit into slices. Mix the mayonnaise with the mango, chutney and lime juice and stir in the chicken and ½ tsp each of salt and pepper.

Divide the mixture between the tortilla wraps, sprinkle with spring onions and rocket, then fold in the bottom third of the wrap and roll up.

Ingredients

4 chicken breasts, skinned

2 tbsp oil

2 ripe mangoes

4 tbsp mayonnaise

2 tbsp mango chutney

juice of 1 lime

12 flour tortilla wraps

4 spring onions (scallions), chopped

1 small bunch rocket (arugula)

salt and pepper

serves 4

40 mins
preparation and cooking time

difficulty

Why not try... adding fish instead of chicken.

Carrot and tomato soup

Method

Carefully heat the oil in a large pan and fry the onion and celery on a medium heat for a few minutes until soft.

Stir in the chopped garlic, carrots and tomatoes and add the stock or water. Turn up the heat and bring it to a boil. Simmer for 15 minutes or until the carrots are cooked.

Whizz the soup in a blender until smooth, then sieve it back into the pan. Add a little bit of salt and pepper and taste it, adding a bit more if needed. Reheat the soup on a low heat, and once it is hot, serve it straight away.

Ingredients

2 tbsp olive oil
1 onion, finely chopped
1 stalk celery, finely chopped
1 clove garlic, chopped
4 large carrots, peeled and chopped
800 g / 2 lbs / 8 cups tomatoes, chopped
1 litre / 35 fl. oz / 4¼ cups
vegetable stock or water

Top tip...
if you like chunky soup, don't blend it and serve straight away.

Macaroni cheese

serves
4

40 mins
preparation and cooking time

difficulty

Method

Bring a pan of water to the boil, and cook the macaroni for 10-12 minutes. Drain the macaroni using a sieve and put it aside.

Heat the oven to 180C (160C fan) 375F, gas 5.

Carefully melt the butter in a saucepan on a medium heat and fry the bacon and onion for 5 minutes. Mix in the flour and cook for 2 minutes then add the milk slowly, stirring all the time.

Turn down the heat for 5 minutes then stir in the cooked macaroni and ¾ of the cheese.

Pour the mixture into individual dishes, sprinkle them with the rest of the cheese, put them on a baking sheet and bake for 15-20 minutes.

Ingredients

500 g / 17.6 oz / 5 cups dried macaroni
1 tbsp butter
2 rashers bacon, chopped
1 onion, finely chopped
2 tbsp flour
500 ml / 17.5 fl. oz / 2 cups milk
200 g / 7 oz / 2 cups cheese, grated

Why not try...
adding sweetcorn or peas to your macaroni.

serves

4

3 hours

40 mins

preparation and cooking time

difficulty

Grilled chicken skewers

Method

Carefully cut the chicken breasts into 4 cm / 1.5" cubes and mix with the lime juice, paprika, cayenne and ketchup. Season with salt and pepper and set aside to marinade for 3 hours.

Cut the avocados in half lengthways, remove the stone and peel off the skin. Chop the avocados and mix with the tomatoes, onion and green pepper.

Stir in the lime juice and coriander and season with salt and pepper.

Ask an adult to help turn on the grill to medium heat. Carefully thread the chicken pieces onto wooden skewers and grill for 8 minutes, turning frequently. The chicken should be cooked through and white.

Ingredients

For the chicken skewers:
4 chicken breasts, skinned
juice of 2 limes
2 tsp ground paprika
½ tsp cayenne pepper
125 ml / 4.3 fl. oz / ½ cup tomato ketchup

For the salad:
2 avocados
4 tomatoes, quartered
1 red onion, chopped
1 green bell pepper, deseeded and chopped
juice of 2 limes
1 tbsp fresh coriander (cilantro), chopped

Top tip...
skewer peppers and onions with your chicken for a tasty veggie treat!

makes

12

2 hours

30 mins

preparation and cooking time

difficulty

Mini pizzas

Method

Put the flour into a bowl with the yeast, salt and sugar and add a bit of water at a time, mixing until the ingredients to form a dough.

Put the dough onto a floured board and knead well for about 10 minutes. Put the dough in a clean bowl, cover with a tea towel and put in a warm place (like a window sill) to rise for 1 hour.

Knead the dough again on a floured board for 5 minutes then let it rise again for 30 minutes.

Heat the oven to 220C (200C fan) 425F, gas 7.

Divide the dough into 12 pieces, roll each out with a floured rolling pin to make circles about 10 cm / 4" diameter and place them on the baking sheet.

Sprinkle each pizza base with grated cheese and cover with the tomatoes and courgettes. Sprinkle with the oregano, a pinch of salt and pepper and some olive oil.

Bake for 15 - 20 minutes.

Ingredients

For the dough:
400 g / 14 oz / 4 cups bread flour
1 sachet dried yeast
1 tsp salt
1 tsp sugar
250 ml / 8 fl. oz / 2½ cups warm water

For the topping:
200 g / 7 oz / 2 cups cheese, grated
400 g / 14 oz / 4 cups cherry tomatoes, halved
2 courgettes (zucchini), thinly sliced
1 tbsp dried oregano
2 tbsp olive oil
6 slices Parma ham, halved
1 bunch rocket (arugula)

Why not try...
adding extra toppings
like ham, pineapple,
or pepperoni.

Homemade fish fingers

difficulty

Method

Cut the fish into strips about 2 cm / ¾" wide. Place the flour, beaten egg and breadcrumbs in to three separate bowls.

With the supervision of an adult, put the oil in a deep pan and heat until it is very hot.

Mix the flour with the salt and pepper. Cover the fish strips with the seasoned flour, then dip the fish strips into the beaten egg and then coat with the bread crumbs.

Fry the fish in batches in the hot oil for 3-4 minutes, or until lightly browned.

Drain on kitchen paper and allow it to cool slightly before serving.

Ingredients

450 g / 1 lb / 4½ cups white fish fillets, cod, haddock or pollack
1 litre / 35 fl. oz / 4½ cups vegetable oil
4 tbsp plain (all-purpose) flour, sifted
2 tsp salt
2 tsp black pepper
2 eggs, beaten
150 g / 5.2 oz / 1½ cups bread crumbs

Top tip...

be very careful when frying fish, oil can be very hot!

Potato and tomato frittata

45 mins
preparation and cooking time

difficulty

Method

Bring a pan of water to the boil and cook the potatoes for 10-12 minutes. Drain them using a sieve and put them aside.

Mix the eggs with the tomatoes and a pinch of salt and pepper. Mix in the chives and parsley.

Cut the potatoes into ½ cm / ¼" slices and gently stir into the egg mixture. Heat the grill to a medium heat.

Being very careful, heat the oil in a 25 cm / 10" frying pan (skillet). After a few minutes, when it is very hot, carefully pour in the egg and potato mixture and turn down the heat a little. Cook for about 4 minutes then put under the grill and continue cooking for a further 3 minutes, or until the eggs are cooked through.

Cut into pie slices and enjoy!

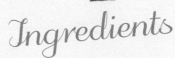

Ingredients

450 g / 1 lb / 4½ cups
waxy new potatoes, scrubbed
4 eggs, beaten
2 tbsp sun-dried tomatoes, chopped
3 tbsp chives, chopped
3 tbsp parsley, chopped
125 ml / 4.3 oz / ½ cup olive oil

Top tip...
any leftover frittata makes a great snack for your lunchbox!

67

Top tip...
meatballs will
freeze really well.

Spaghetti with meatballs

difficulty

Method

To make the meatballs, mix the mince, onion, herbs, salt, pepper and egg together in a bowl and roll the mix into 16 balls.

Heat a little oil in a pan on a medium heat and gently cook the meatballs for 5 minutes, making sure they don't stick.

To make the tomato sauce, heat the oil in a pan on a medium heat and fry the onion and garlic for 5 minutes, or until soft. Add the tomatoes and the meatballs and turn the heat down for 20 minutes, stirring from time to time. To make sure it doesn't dry out, try adding a little hot water.

Stir in the sugar and tomato paste and a pinch of salt and pepper. Remove the pan from the heat.

Put a large pan of water on to boil and cook the spaghetti for 10–12 minutes. Drain the spaghetti using a sieve and serve with the meatballs.

Ingredients

For the meatballs:
2 tbsp olive oil
1 onion, chopped
450 g / 1 lb / 4½ cups minced beef
1 tsp dried mixed herbs
1 egg, beaten
2 tbsp oil, for frying

For the tomato sauce:
2 tbsp olive oil
1 onion, finely chopped
1 clove garlic, chopped
400 g / 14 oz / 4 cups
chopped tomatoes
1 tsp sugar
1 tbsp tomato paste

To serve:
400 g / 14 oz / 4 cups spaghetti

difficulty

Baked potatoes with cheese

Method

Heat the oven to 200C (180C fan) 400F, gas 6.

Rub the potatoes with the oil and salt and bake on the middle shelf of the oven for about an hour, or until they feel soft.

Let the potatoes cool a little then cut each in half lengthways. Carefully scoop out the cooked potato and mix with the cheese, sweetcorn and butter.

Put the potato and cheese mixture into the potato skin shells, place on a baking sheet and bake for 15 minutes.

Ingredients

4 large baking potatoes, washed
1 tbsp vegetable oil
1 tbsp salt
200 g / 7 oz / 2 cups cheese, grated
200 g / 7 oz / 2 cups sweetcorn, canned
1 tbsp butter

Why not try...
adding tuna or baked beans to your potatoes.

serves

4

1 hour

15 mins

preparation and cooking time

difficulty

Red peppers with mince stuffing

Method

Bring a pan of water to the boil, and cook the rice for 10-12 minutes. Drain it using a sieve and put it aside.

Heat the oven to 200C (180C fan) 400F, gas 6.

Carefully heat the oil in a wide pan to a medium heat and fry the spring onions. Add the garlic and chilli and cook for 2 minutes. Stir in the beef and fry on a high heat for 5 minutes, or until the meat has browned.

Mix the mince with the cooked rice, mustard, ketchup and eggs, and a pinch of salt and pepper.

Wash the peppers, cut a lid from each and remove the seeds.

Place the peppers on a baking tray and fill with the mince mixture. Put the lids on and bake in a preheated oven for 30-40 minutes.

Ingredients

100 g / 3.5 oz / 1 cup rice
2 tbsp olive oil
1 bunch spring onions (scallions), chopped
2 cloves garlic, chopped
1 chilli, deseeded, chopped
450 g / 1 lb / 4½ cups minced beef
8 red bell peppers
1 tsp hot mustard
1 tbsp ketchup
2 eggs, beaten

Top tip...
for a delicious dinner,
serve with chunky chips
(see page 14).

Desserts

Top tip...
leave the trifle in the
refrigerator overnight
to help it set.

Strawberry trifle

serves
4

1 hour
15 mins

preparation and cooking time

difficulty

Method

For the strawberry jelly, make the jelly according to the packet instructions and chill in the fridge overnight.

For the vanilla cream, put 200 ml of the milk into a pan and bring to a boil on a medium heat. Mix the cornflour and vanilla extract with the sugar to make a smooth paste with the remaining milk. Stir this into the boiling milk and cook for 2 minutes until thickened.

Remove the pan from the heat and leave it to cool, stirring. Whisk the cream until thick and fold it into the cold vanilla milk.

Gently warm the jam. If the sponge is one large cake, break it up into smaller chunks or slice thinly. Spread the jam over the cake and put it into individual cups.

Put a few orange segments and strawberries in, then a spoonful of strawberry jelly. Divide the vanilla cream between the glasses and top it with the remaining strawberries.

Ingredients

plain vanilla sponge cake
strawberry jam
1 pack strawberry jelly

For the vanilla cream:
350 ml / 11.8 fl. oz / 1½ cups milk
2 tbsp cornflour (cornstarch)
1 tsp vanilla extract
2 tbsp sugar
100 ml / 3.4 fl. oz / 1½ cups cream

In addition:
400 g / 14 oz / 4 cups strawberries, sliced
1 orange, peeled and segmented

makes

8

25 mins

preparation and cooking time

difficulty

Toffee apples on sticks

Method

Wipe the apples well to remove any waxy coating, otherwise the toffee won't stick. Remove the stalks and put a stick or a wooden skewer in each stalk end.

Carefully heat the sugar, butter and water in a pan over a low heat until it is all dissolved. Bring to a boil and cook for a few minutes.

Remove from the heat and stir in the colouring.

Dip the apples into the toffee, swirling them around until coated. Place them on non-stick baking paper and allow them to set.

Ingredients

8 eating apples
450 g / 15.8 oz / 4½ cups sugar
110 g / 3.9 oz / 1 cup butter
2 tbsp water
red food colouring

Top tip...

eat them within a few hours, or the apples will become sticky.

serves

4

5 hours

20 mins

preparation and cooking time

difficulty

Raspberry yoghurt ice-cream

Method

Put the icing sugar and raspberries into a food processor and blend until it is smooth.

Add the honey and yoghurt and blend it again, until all of the ingredients are smoothly mixed.

Spoon the mixture into a freezer-proof container, seal and freeze the ice-cream for at least 5 hours.

To serve, dip an ice-cream scoop into a jug of hot water and scoop the ice-cream into bowls. Decorate with fresh raspberries.

Ingredients

50 g / 1.7 oz / ½ cup
icing (confectioners') sugar, sifted
300 g / 10.5 oz / 3 cups
frozen raspberries
4 tbsp runny honey
500 g / 17.6 oz / 5 cups natural yoghurt

To garnish:
12 fresh raspberries

Top tip...
the longer the ice-cream
is in the freezer for,
the better it will set.

Top tip...
try dipping marshmallows,
brazil nuts, or biscuits
into the chocolate.

Chocolate fondue with fruit and honey bread

serves

4

1 hour

40 mins

preparation and cooking time

difficulty

Method

Mix the honey, milk, mixed spice and cinnamon together in a bowl and pour over the bread, allowing it to soak for 10 minutes. Chop the bread up into chunks. Carefully halve the strawberries and slice the bananas. Place all the fruit and the honey bread on a plate, ready to serve. Spear onto wooden skewers.

For the chocolate fondue, place all the ingredients into a pan over a low heat and stir until it has melted. Remove from the heat and allow the chocolate mixture to cool for a moment.

Pour the melted chocolate mixture into a bowl and serve with the fresh fruit and honey bread.

Ingredients

For the chocolate fondue:
350 g / 12.3 oz / 3½ cups dark or milk chocolate
150 ml / 5 fl. oz / ⅔ cup cream
75 g / 2.6 oz / ¾ cups dark brown sugar
1 tbsp cocoa powder
1 tsp vanilla extract

For the honey bread:
300 ml / 10 fl. oz / 1¼ cups runny honey
4 slices wholemeal bread, crusts removed,
2 tsp mixed spice
1 tsp cinnamon
2 tbsp milk

Fruit for dipping:
grapes
bananas, sliced
strawberries, halved

Bread pudding with raspberries

serves 4

40 mins

preparation and cooking time

difficulty

Method

Heat the oven to 180C (155 fan) 350F, gas 4.
Rub a little bit of butter inside 4 extra-large coffee
cups (or small dessert bowls).

Beat the eggs with the cream and sugar,
using a wooden spoon, until it is smooth.

Butter the bread slices and cut into small pieces.
Arrange half the bread, buttered side up, in the
cups. Scatter over half the raspberries.

Top with the remaining bread and raspberries.
Pour over the egg mixture and leave to stand
for 10 minutes, for the bread to soak up some
of the mixture.

Bake for 20-25 minutes until puffy and golden.

Ingredients

2 eggs
400 ml / 13.5 fl. oz / 1¾ cups cream
2 tbsp sugar
2 tbsp butter
6 slices stale white bread, crusts removed
250 g / 8.8 oz / 2½ cups fresh raspberries

Top tip...
serve the puddings warm,
with extra custard.

serves

4

25 mins

preparation and cooking time

difficulty

Pancakes with jam

Method

Mix together the flour and milk until smooth. Add the eggs, sugar, vanilla and a pinch of salt. Leave to rest for 20 minutes.

Heat a little butter in a pan on a medium heat and add a ladle, or 2 large tablespoonfuls, of batter. Cook for 1-2 minutes until golden brown.

Carefully flip the pancake and cook for the same amount of time on the other side. Place it on a plate and repeat with the rest of the batter.

Serve with jam and a sprinkling of sugar.

Ingredients

150 g / 5.3 oz / 1½ cups flour
300 ml / 10 fl. oz / 1⅓ cups milk
3 eggs
2 tsp sugar
3 drops vanilla extract
salt
50 g / 1.7 oz / ½ cup butter, for frying
sugar
strawberry jam

Why not try...

sugar and lemon, or chocolate spread, instead of jam for a delicious treat.

serves

4

15 mins

preparation and cooking time

difficulty

Fruit salad with honey

Method

Combine the fruits in a large bowl.

Mix the honey and lemon juice and pour over the fruit. Mix it well to coat the fruit and chill before serving.

Ingredients

200 g / 7 oz / 2 cups strawberries, halved if large
2 oranges, peeled and segmented
160 g / 5.6 oz / 1½ cups green, seedless grapes
110 g / 3.9 oz / 1 cup black, seedless grapes
250 g / 8.8 oz / 1½ cups melon, cubed
5 tbsp honey
1 tsp lemon juice

Top tip...

add a squeeze of lemon juice to stop the fruit from going brown.

Eton mess

preparation and cooking time

15 mins

Method

Place the raspberries in a bowl and mash gently with a fork.

Use an electric whisk to whisk the cream until it is softly peaking. Try turning the bowl upside down and if the egg whites are firm enough and don't drip, they're ready.

Gently fold in the raspberries and the broken up meringue pieces. Spoon it into glasses or bowls and serve.

difficulty

Ingredients

500 g / 17.6 oz / 5 cups raspberries
1 tbsp icing (confectioners') sugar
500 ml / 16.9 fl. oz / 2 cups whipping cream
110 g / 3.9 oz / 1 cup ready-made meringues, broken into pieces

Why not try...

adding chopped nuts
or coconut flakes
for extra crunch!

Fruity kebabs with raspberry purée

serves

4

25 mins

preparation and cooking time

difficulty

Method

Skewer the fruit onto wooden kebab sticks. Puree half the raspberries with the lemon juice in a blender. Pour the puree through a sieve, into a small dipping bowl.

Carefully heat the butter and oil in a pan, on a low to medium heat. Grill the kebabs, until lightly browned on both sides. Dust with icing sugar.

Serve the kebabs with the raspberry puree to dip in and the rest of the raspberries.

Top tip...

try cooking the kebabs on the grill or barbeque with the help of an adult.

Ingredients

1 mango, peeled and chopped into cubes
½ pineapple, peeled and chopped into cubes
300 g / 10.5 oz / 3 cups fresh raspberries
1 tbsp lemon juice
1 tbsp butter
1 tsp olive oil
2 tbsp icing (confectioners') sugar

serves

4

1 hour

25 mins

preparation and cooking time

difficulty

Chocolate mousse

Method

Place the chocolate in a heatproof bowl, over a pan of simmering water on a low to medium heat, stirring while it melts. Once it is smooth and liquid, remove from the heat and allow it to cool slightly.

Meanwhile, beat the egg yolks. In a separate bowl, whisk the egg whites until they form soft peaks. Try turning the bowl upside down and if the egg whites are firm enough and don't drip, they're ready.

Stir the beaten egg yolks into the melted chocolate. Gently fold in the egg whites until the mixture is smooth.

Divide evenly between individual glasses and chill for 1 hour. You can decorate with shavings of white chocolate, by using a grater.

Ingredients

175 g | 6.2 oz | 1¾ cups dark chocolate
4 eggs, separated
75 g | 2.6 oz | ¾ cup white chocolate

Top tip...

try using an electric whisk for the egg whites, to make it easier.

Index